TRIAL OF A JUDGE

TRIAL OF A
JUDGE

A TRAGEDY IN FIVE ACTS BY

STEPHEN SPENDER

RANDOM HOUSE · NEW YORK

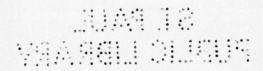

To T. A. R. H.

The world wears your image on the surface
And judges, as always, the looks and the behaviour
Moving upon the social glass of silver;
But I plunged through those mirrored rays
Where eye remarks eye from the outside,
Into your hidden inner self and bore
As my self-love your hopes and failure,
The small flagged island on which I would have died.

Drowned in your life, I there encountered death
Which claimed you for a greater history
Where the free won, though many won too late.
We being afraid, I made my hand a path
Into this separate peace which is no victory
Nor general peace, but our escape from fate.

CHARACTERS

THE JUDGE
THE JUDGE'S WIFE
HUMMELDORF
PETRA'S MOTHER
PETRA'S BROTHER
THE FIANCÉE
A COMMUNIST (THIRD RED)
FIVE BLACK PRISONERS (BLACK CHORUS)
A FASCIST TROOP LEADER
TWO FASCISTS (SIXTH BLACK AND SEVENTH BLACK)
JEWISH DOCTOR PRISONER
CHORUS OF RED PRISONERS

Act One

ILLUSION AND UNCERTAINTY

[SCENE: *The edge of a wood in the garden of the Palace of Justice. Through the trees are discernible the lights of the Palace and the Square onto which it faces. Lights and colours suggesting illusion and uncertainty. Action suggesting that this act is a dream in the Judge's mind.*]

[*Enter the* JUDGE, *from the trial in which he has just passed the death sentence on Petra's murderers. He is agitated. Dressed in court robes.*]

JUDGE. 'Regret,' let me remember, 'Regret.'
What did I speak? 'Regret.'
Every word was true. Not one word
Does my conscience take back.
Yet to call murder murder is a kind of killing,
Perhaps which makes me their souls' murderer.
The carotid artery was severed,
Petra's body mangled out of recognition.
What could I say, except assert
That my famous gentleness, changed to outrage,
Would stamp their lives out with a kind of pleasure?
'Judge not, lest ye be judged'—that means nothing,
    I suppose,
Unless that, in killing, judges may not damn men's
    souls

9

—Old tags echo in the ear.
Even the masked frock-coated executioner,
With his naked surgery, kills but judges not.
The surgeon should have hands to pity
Gangrened flesh the scalpel cuts.
Yes, yes; but what I said I disposed over their exe-
    cution
Not to their souls but at their deeds
To a listening world which must be warned.
Why do I remember these things? I suppose
A lawyer's a man well-trained in memory
Of cases, precedent, repartee, speeches,
So now my words like birds fly after me.
What did I say? 'Regret.'

   [*Savagely, echoing not the words but the im-
   plication of his speech to the Court, he turns
   round and addresses an at first invisible* CHOR-
   US, *who gradually come forward from under
   the trees, until they stand round, facing him,
   as much the accusers as the accused. The
   whole scene vaguely recalls the arrangement
   of the Court. The* JUDGE *stands on a slightly
   higher level of the proscenium.*]

We are driven to violence by violence
Of groups hidden in crowds, like a ripe core
Packed with black seeds driving outwards.
You have loosed inciting leaflets: with crimes
Done under covering night, you would melt
All confidence in rules to one searing rule
Of organized terror. You know the law
Makes hourly statements like electric advertise-
    ments

In city squares—those man-tall golden letters
You have stood in falsely with false legality
When practising sharp-shooting at the edge of
    woods
—When severing the life of this Jew.
I do regretfully
Announce a change made in the law
Which, acting retrogressively, makes political
    murder
Punishable with death:
Regret. Let me remember, regret.
No, I am glad.
To stamp you out, we will change the laws to traps
In every street
Common as traps of drains under your feet.

> [*The* BLACK CHORUS *is composed of Five
> Prisoners. They are too idealised to be dis-
> missed simply as bullies; yet they suggest at
> once the accused and the accusers, the op-
> pressed and the oppressors. First, their voices
> mutter in the background, as though they
> were a memory in depths of the Judge's own
> unconscious mind. Later, they come to the
> front of the stage, until, at the end of the
> scene, they stand between the audience and
> the* JUDGE.]

FIRST BLACK PRISONER. Our orders were to shoot Petra.
JUDGE. [*as though recalling the voice of the Prosecutor*].
    Who ordered you?
SECOND BLACK PRISONER. We met each night
    Where we could wear our uniforms, in our own
        cellars,

11

And there with the town's list before us, we
Pricked every name of Pole or Jew.
THIRD BLACK PRISONER. Petra came first: he was a
    Polish Jew.
FOURTH BLACK PRISONER. And a Marxist as well.
FIRST BLACK PRISONER. We met on Thursday night
    and motored out
From Beuthen to Potempa by the road:
Skidding—spark-showers at corners—we did not
    hug
The cover of blackness, but as we
Do here, and always shall do,
Awakened dumb houses with our slogans
And let the fumbling secret lovers know
Loving is trash to those who strike a light
Of liberating fire with their revenge.
FIFTH BLACK PRISONER. The gross-lipped fawn-eyed
    nigger-skinned
Hook-nosed intellectual Petra
Snored in a stenching windowless
Sty with his mother and his brother.
FOURTH BLACK PRISONER. In unmanly filth of poverty,
    he lacked
Food, candle and fire.
Inferior of physique, he coughed
His guts out, whilst about the room he crept
And wove his plots from sterile cleverness.
To judge from books and papers spread around,
Petra was like an angel, without food
Existing singly from his light of mind.
FIFTH BLACK PRISONER. We dragged him screaming
Out of the straw bed by the heels.

I shot him, stripped. Then we stamped on him
And kicked his face in.
SECOND BLACK PRISONER. Although we thought he
coughed up all his blood,
When we struck him, there was enough blood.
JUDGE. O, let collectors and doctors recognise
Here a rarity, like Pandy's disease.
The carotid artery was severed
Such violence is a diamond.
THIRD BLACK PRISONER. If you want proof
That him alone we abhorred as a spy
And murdered through our racial privilege, re-
member
We spared two witnesses
His lunatic mother and his brother.
FIRST BLACK PRISONER. Europe is a jungle where the
tiger
Vegetable silence breaks
—A sun through branches.
As the spurned ground of all earth's disk
Which man advancing tramples,
Slaying grass, axing forests, blasting rock,
Rejecting the inanimate as trash,
So are weak men to the strong.
Soft waters sift away whole soils,
Sentimental moons madden the dogs,
And the effeminate Jew rustling subtly
Through corridors as a brook through reeds,
Our strength saps.
FIFTH BLACK PRISONER. But we are slayers, springing
Upon the weak from topmost branches,
Killing the okapi, the kid, the pascal lamb.

First Black Prisoner. Let the biped stand, let the
          nordic
     Sunhaired head be matched against cloud drifts
     And the whip hand crack the lightning
     Canine and eye teeth laugh in the sun's face.
     His flags never dip except for night
     Or their momentary mutual salute
     Or to utter surrender—yet Western Man
     Less proud than happy standards of bunting
     Is barked by dogs, governed by servants,
     Gutted by the Jew, reproached by niggers.
     Return, O gentlemen of the field, to your primary
          hunting!
Judge. Since once in my country
     Such a murder is done, and there are eleven million
     Who will applaud the doers, we approach
     Smoking fields of chaos where
     The integral mind melts in collected
     Panic and cruelty. Standards of justice topple like
          masts
     And what's called right seems a battered tin
     On banks of rubbish where lie
     Flanges of history's once competent machines.
     Regard today
     Whose paper figure on the calendar
     Has shaken the traditional libraries
     And still will wing like seed into the ground
     To produce from the instant a generation of chaos
     Unless some signal act of anger
     Strike out these words of murder . . .
     To fortify my will
     I summon Petra's mother and his brother.

14

FIFTH BLACK PRISONER. The words of Poles, who, when
    our country
    Knew defeat
FIRST BLACK PRISONER.   —the barriers smashed
SECOND BLACK PRISONER. The soldiers in rags, the
    young hollow-boned,
    The coinage a torrent, our credit dust,
    Crept in to eat our ruin.
THIRD BLACK PRISONER. And the words of Jews—
FOURTH BLACK PRISONER. Their roots suck our mines,
    our factories
FIFTH BLACK PRISONER. Our girls, our boys, our industry,
    They secretly channel our blood abroad
    While their gaping mouths as red as our wounds
    Hover in cars or plaster our cafés.
FOURTH BLACK PRISONER. And the words of Com-
    munists—
THIRD BLACK PRISONER. Machines without a nation:
FIFTH BLACK PRISONER. Millions of bodies the same:
    millions of minds
    Colourless as the Asiatic plains.
CHORUS OF BLACK PRISONERS. No, we are young and
    die for it, but
    The patriot who loves his field shall flourish.
    He will plant his wheat with the same hand
    As drives aggressors from his land.
JUDGE [prosecuting, as before]. Let
    The dead man's brother and his mother speak.
        [Enter the MOTHER and PETRA'S BROTHER.
        The mother, a Catholic, wears long nunnish
        mourning. Petra's brother, is in mechanic's
        blue dungarees.]

MOTHER. Are you the Judge? Sir, will you discover
    The murderers of my son?
JUDGE [*raising her with a gesture which is really his own
        self-pity*].
    Is this woman then a Jewess?
        [*Answering in his rôle of prosecutor, as be-
        fore.*]
    No.
    Her room
    Carpetless
    Lightless bare walls
    Smelling of stale cardboard
    Was papered
    With photographs
    Of holy paintings and images
    Cut from the newspapers.
    Is it true, Frau Petra, as these prisoners declare,
        that your son was an atheist?
MOTHER. Now God has forgiven him.
PETRA'S BROTHER. Oh—
JUDGE [*prosecuting, as before*]. Tell us how your son
        came to die!
MOTHER. We went to bed early, for my son was a good
        son
    Causing me no anxiety with late hours but staying
        at home;
    Going to rest at dark and rising to read by the dawn
    He was what you might call a studious one.
    Now I pray God to pour Hell fire upon his murder-
        ers
    Who, with a dark lantern—five there were—
    Broke in with sticks and revolvers on our slumber

16

—Found nothing to steal except my solitary trea-
sure
My son, my son. Sir, well I remember
That night, the hottest night of this summer, how
He coughed, so that if at all of evil I dreamt,
It was to pray he might die peacefully.
PETRA'S BROTHER. These five broke on our sleep. I
thought
They were drunks. When I leapt up
To save my brother, one's leaded truncheon
Dazzled my eyes with a blazing star.
That the harm they planned my brother
Was worse than drunken play turned brutal
You all can witness.
[Here TWO ATTENDANTS *reveal the body of
Petra laid out on a table under lamps.*]
MOTHER. Once this pale-faced child, my son, the slag
hill
Each morning climbed, serious with his satchel.
He was mature and gentle, like a girl.
PETRA'S BROTHER. Do not—as beggars do—
Hold his wounds under their noses
And change him entirely to horror, pity or frank
money.
MOTHER. His touch was the last companion for such
wish
I have for life left in decaying flesh—
PETRA'S BROTHER. Oh
So far from gentle, he is the danger
His murderers and those who gave them orders
Still fear. They did not kill to kill
My already dying brother, stoned

17

By starvation, hunger heavier
Than a grave's alleviating weight of soil:
For visibly he belonged to dark
Death, like lean tendrils
Of sunless plants, prophesying shroud worms.
They shot only his face
That's still the face of what he is:
Their leaden bullets against a knife edge
Of steel, have tried to turn the blade:
But instantly when he died, the entire knife
Of what he thought and strove, glued to my hand.
He's dead. His living was one word
Influencing surrounding speech
Of a crowd's life, printless until
The words of all this time are frozen
By all our deaths into the winter library
Where life continually flows into books.
For us the blood still melts
We breathe a ripe or sparse or torturing air
And are the cursive act of history
Moving with fever, like distraction
In waves. I with dead sight
Of him you killed—with his undying will
Your bullets shot at—read
In your faces and your actions
Present history, and, in the reading, I shall write.
Myself a word amongst existing words
Reading your words, I see in them death's orders.
I tell you, this impartial judge
Weaker than his own justice, shall smile
And pardon Petra's murderers.
These prisoners, Petra's murderers,

Shall sit upon a bench to judge this judge;
And where my brother's life has printed
The contradiction to your world of lies
I'll stamp his truth again with my own breath,
Yes, even with my death.

MOTHER. Please do not heed him, he's dangerous,
But hear all our history, how we are harmless.
My husband was a Jew and it was twelve years ago
That, being hated there, we left Poland, our
    country.
My two sons were then children whom the migra-
    tory train
Carried crawling inside, with other emigrants,
    through
Freezing smoke of that winter night. We experi-
    enced
Not kindness, not death, but many small daggers
First of frost, then of hunger, through our bodies.
The mournful telegraph wires which watched our
    travelling
From town to town have never worn birds
To sing our harvest in: secret eye never watched us
Profit from this country's loss to become the right
    target
For hatred of those who now hit us. Gentlemen,
You who carved furrows through my son, as waste-
    fully
As if one intolerable night of flight
Had passed with engine wheels not over his mind
    alone
But also across his sensible eyes—
Oh, had you leave now to analyse his ruined flesh

You would find his bones marrowless from a
    starved childhood,
His blood impure as your country's debased cur-
    rency.
Suffering's suffrage had balloted him
That alas chose the people of our new-chosen
    country,
Has driven them mad now in their hatred of
    strangers
. . . If you have any pity, spare a shilling for me.
    [*Exit, walking slowly across the stage past the*
    CHORUS, *who at once revile her and contemp-*
    tuously throw a few coppers.]
JUDGE. Here in the Court of my mind, I invoke
    Not only Petra's murderers and the mother
    Of him and his brother, but her
    Who carries in her body his child.
    [*Enter* FIANCÉE *at back of stage, high up (at*
    the same level as the balcony in Act III and
    the gables in Act V), under smothered rays
    from the Palace. She is small, pretty, fair,
    dressed in a skirt and red woollen jumper. The
    JUDGE *stands to the front of the stage, apart,*
    as he watches her and PETRA'S BROTHER *speak*
    together.]
FIANCÉE [*to* PETRA'S BROTHER]. I will be the mother of
    your brother's child.
    Can you take care of me?
PETRA'S BROTHER. I must go away.
FIANCÉE. Where will you go?
PETRA'S BROTHER. To follow Petra.
FIANCÉE. Petra is dead.

PETRA'S BROTHER. The frontier which I cross is that
    Bombed impassable road within
    Easy reach of trained machine guns, which
    Divides banks and cathedrals from the slums.
    Look up where wealth's Gibraltar stares across
    The workers' salt undifferentiated, fretting sea.
    There the rich build in simple stone which holds
    Cells of our blood and sweat transformed to gold;
    And yet I thought all men were kind, until
    Their naked guns blasted my brother.
    Dear, where I must go I'll go alone
    To suffer no morbid wounds from seeing
    A home and children starve. I must be poor.
    To cross that frontier all I need declare
    Is I have nothing and I give my life
    To those with nothing but their lives.
FIANCÉE. I'll follow you, although we snatch our peace.
PETRA'S BROTHER. From death, from death—
JUDGE. [apart at front of stage]. The lovers on their light
        and subtle hill,
    The dancers in the stage's polished window,
    Are buried in my boyhood's memory.
FIANCÉE. Between death and life
    Our love shall create a link.
PETRA'S BROTHER. Yes, curled in your body, my broth-
        er's child.
FIANCÉE. We'll tear love—
PETRA'S BROTHER. From the iron assertions of the
        time—
JUDGE [apart]. They turn like little wheels of clocks: the
        hair spring
    Girl circling around her central jewel

21

The trigger sir, the arrow regulator.
FIANCÉE. Between the slogans of comrades—
PETRA'S BROTHER. After the ten hours' day in the
        factory—
JUDGE [apart]. O, their wishes were horses on which I
        rode!
I awaited fulfilment from the sexual rose
When all the choric petals were unfurled.
FIANCÉE. We'll force love—
PETRA'S BROTHER. To grow in improbable places—
FIANCÉE. Under the street doorways—
PETRA'S BROTHER. The yawning railway arches—
FIANCÉE. One night of release in the park—
PETRA'S BROTHER. Under the trees blossoming with
        electric flowers—
JUDGE [apart]. If there is love or any dancer's art
    To restore symmetry now, it must be stronger
    Than small brass wheels—I must have cranes
    To lift stone weights, or love
    Powerful enough to run a country on.
PETRA'S BROTHER and FIANCÉE.
    Petra's child will be fruit of our will.
        [FIANCÉE and PETRA'S BROTHER turn to go.
        Before they do so, whilst she is turned away
        from the stage, he speaks in an impassioned
        voice.]
PETRA'S BROTHER. Here I have a voice impassioned,
    Here I have a life disputed and indignant,
    Here I have a message, here I have a life.[1]

      [1] Aqui tengo una voz enardecida,
      aqui tengo una vida combatida y airada,
      aqui tengo un rumor, aqui tengo una vida.
                    Miguel Hernandez.

[*Exeunt* PETRA's BROTHER *and* FIANCÉE. *The*
JUDGE *stands over Petra's corpse and address-*
es the CHORUS *with the ritualistic passion of*
the law.]

JUDGE. After the war, after the years of starving, after
    chains
  That weighed us down with debt,
  We look across the gulf of chaos,
  Of sporadic fire, wastrel opinion
  Armed with guns: there, responsibility
  Alone of burdens, was fallen from us.
  But now I say at last the change is rung
  Whoever having authority
  Errs from the centre of collected powers
  Pointed into the State, is friend to murderers
  And to that wandering outward fringe of rebel
  Disintegrators.
  The law is better guns and prisons
  Than cracks across our country's discipline.
  Therefore my ruling is that death,
  As ordered by the decree, fall on you.

CHORUS OF BLACK PRISONERS. The people hear our
    voice
  The people will change this sentence and make
    sentences
  Other than this.

JUDGE. The corpse of Petra is a witness
  His wounds are mouths speaking red words.

FIRST BLACK PRISONER. The life of Petra was an ulcer
  We cut out of our country's body.

JUDGE. The son-deprived womb of Petra's mother
  The fatherless womb of his unborn child

23

Cry that their love was murdered.

SECOND BLACK PRISONER. The Jew-bearing womb of
      Petra's mother
The Jew-debauched womb of his bride
Were the theatres of our cleansing operation.

JUDGE. A word is planted in his brother's mouth
A will is planted in his brother's mind.

THIRD BLACK PRISONER. We'll root the word out of his
      mouth
And cut the will out of his mind.

JUDGE. A spectre rises from Petra's body
A spectre crying that my justice
Must die or fortify itself.

FOURTH BLACK PRISONER. That is the signal for our
      attack!
When liberal justice whines of violence
Power flies to those with the right of might.

JUDGE. Petra's murder
Printed in a million newspapers
Torn and carried by the wind,
Tugs like entrails on the blackthorn
And fouls the edges of the city
Where greenness first begins.

FIRST BLACK PRISONER. Our martyrdom
Blazoned on a million sheets of paper
Is a trumpet blowing
Millions to the cause
Of heroes who warn the people's enemies
With this exemplary, just, horrible death.

JUDGE. Then, for the sake of such a peace
As still does mantle sunset villages
Where the heart may love and rest,

24

Which still to Europe I may restore,
And, for the survival of a vision
Within the human memory
Of absolute justice accepted by consent;
And for those margins of possibility
In our free actions, which open doors
To imagination and to music;
And, for the sake of my own integrity
Which drives me to an insupportable air
Where the earth, killed by tyrants,
Is cut away from under me—
SECOND BLACK PRISONER. Then, for the sake of an
        indivisible nation
Embossed beneath one iron will;
And, for a conquering army led
To banish pity and thought;
And, for the purified blood like a tide
Streaming through heroic children;
And, to throw off our present chains
With a gesture which is freedom
Proclaiming that our might is right,
We rise against your laws.
        [*Threatening they rise up between the* JUDGE
        and the footlights, hiding him from the audi-
        ence.]
JUDGE [*retreating*]. My truth will win.
CHORUS OF BLACK PRISONERS. The people hear our
        voice.
The people will change this sentence and make
        sentences
Other than this.

CURTAIN

25

Act Two

THE SMALL SCENE

[SCENE: *A room in the Palace of Justice. Bare and whitewashed with folding doors on right, leading through a passage directly to the Law Court. Another door, left. In front a window leading out onto the balcony. The* JUDGE's WIFE, *a fat, masterly invalid of sixty, is talking to* HUMMELDORF, *a minister of the Government.* HUMMELDORF *is white-whiskered: he is in morning dress.*]

WIFE [*standing in front of the folding doors*]. No, no, I forbid you to see him. As his wife I put my foot down. A woman in my position doesn't expect any gratitude (I don't even ask my husband to waste one moment of his just, well-used time on me); but I can at least do my duty. How do you expect that justice would be CREATED in this Court if I wasn't here to protect my husband?

HUMMELDORF [*agitated*]. You must please believe me, I have come here on a very important matter. It is a question of whether the judge will agree to the reprieve of the prisoners who were condemned to death for the murder of a Polish Jew called Petra.

WIFE. Reprieve? Reprieve? When I've not been able to sleep for a week on account of the trouble these two cases have given my husband? Now that he's brought himself to condemn them, must he go through all that mental struggle again, a struggle which brought him to the very threshold of death,

27

when offering these worthless creatures to their Maker, in order to fetch them back? No, Mr Home Secretary, if you'd comforted that man, lying by his side night after night, you'd know that those who have made him suffer so much can NEVER be reprieved. The President of the State has his answer from ME: there will be NO reprieve.

HUMMELDORF. Of course the President of the State has the power to over-rule any decision, however exemplary, made by your husband. But, in this case, for the sake of the nation—

WIFE [*sitting down heavily in an armchair*]. Mr Hummeldorf, if you have any consideration whatever, please don't TORTURE me with these requests any more. [*Drawing a rug over herself.*] As a matter of fact I'm an invalid and I simply haven't the strength. . . .

> [*The doors are thrown open, from within. The* JUDGE's VOICE *is heard speaking, with intense feeling, from the Court.*]

JUDGE's VOICE. But now, I say the change is rung
Whoever being a Judge
Errs from the centre of collected powers
Pointed into the State, is friend to murderers
And to that wandering outward fringe of rebel
Disintegrators.

> [*The* VOICE *is drowned in murmurs. Then there follows the noise of the Court dispersing.*]

WIFE [*to Hummeldorf*]. Please leave me. Allow me at least to have a few words with my husband alone.

HUMMELDORF. But, madam, I entreat you, there is a

28

grave crisis. I must insist on speaking to your husband. Only he can now save the government—

WIFE. *I* shall arrange everything, Mr Hummeldorf. My husband is an inspiring idealist but it is not he who makes decisions. How often in history does the last word of a great and splendid man lie with an unknown woman—his wife. And how little does history, written by men, recognise it! I shall call you in when I have spoken to my husband.

HUMMELDORF. Where shall I wait?

WIFE [*pointing to door on left*]. In there, in there.

[*Exit* HUMMELDORF, *left.*]

[*Enter* JUDGE.]

JUDGE. It is a judicial crime. The President of the State should reprieve them.

WIFE [*astonished*]. Who?

JUDGE. The three Communist prisoners whom I have just sentenced to death.

WIFE [*indignantly*]. Communists! And why should *they* be released, may I ask?

JUDGE [*pacing up and down*]. Because the sentence is unjust. Consider the whole situation. Since our country's defeat in the War, a new generation has arisen. We, the older generation, secretly hoping that the young will regain what we lost, and conniving at a betrayal of the Treaty which we signed, have allowed these boys to acquire arms. Now, suddenly, a new law is passed, making it illegal to carry firearms: so that when a street fight takes place in which some of these young people are attacked by the Black Troops—or even by the police—I am asked to sentence them to the same

29

death penalty as I passed on Petra's murderers, yet
this morning's case was a very different one from
the planned bestiality of Petra's murder.

WIFE. I'm angry, really angry, that you bother about
young people. What have they been since the
War? Selfish, lazy, inconsiderate, self-indulgent,
critical of those who are better and older than
themselves. The best of the whole lot were killed
in the War. Who cared then about the justice of
millions of men being killed?
No, your heart did not break
When the world cracked
And our country's dear sons, like blood corpuscles,
Clotted to make a scar
Across the European gap.

JUDGE [*gently*]. Remember the mothers and fathers of
these three young men.

WIFE. O, I'm glad, I'm glad I had no children. I hate
this younger generation who are discontented, too
lazy to work, ungrateful to those who slave day and
night for them. They have no respect, reverence
nor decency. I wish that there would be another
war, like a great bonfire on which to cast these
faggots.

JUDGE. We teach our children killing. When their
Generosity—bred in tender valleys
Unplundered by the latest robber barons—
Rises against lessons of death, it speaks
Through mouths of revolvers which we taught.
Then, still to maintain the gentlemanly cycle
Of smiling disaster, we execute
Their spiritual will armed against war.

30

WIFE. No, I am on the side of MEN who are still willing to die for their country. The children of my
thought are those brave young men who murdered
Petra; they were patriots; they were willing to lose
their lives in order to rid the country of a rat.

JUDGE. My children would live and die for a world in
which such acts of brutality were impossible.

WIFE [*bitterly*]. Then your children killed my children
in the womb. We are childless.

JUDGE. We can each fight for the lives of those who
might have been our children.

WIFE [*rising from her chair*]. Then I shall fight for the
lives of Petra's murderers. They are *my* children.
And I'll show whose side I am on. [*She walks over
to the door and opens it.*] Mr Hummeldorf, my
husband will be glad to see you.

[*Enter* HUMMELDORF.]

JUDGE. The Home Secretary—Mr Hummeldorf! To
what do I owe this honour?

HUMMELDORF, [*pompously to* JUDGE]. I have come to
deliver a message of appreciation to you from the
President of the State, in recognition of the truly
awe-inspiring warning which you delivered yesterday to the armed Black bands. The President, in
his own words, appreciates in your speech almost
an excess of impartiality.

JUDGE. Well?

HUMMELDORF [*turning away and then producing press
cuttings from his coat pocket*]. You know, sir, that
the patriot leader has sent a telegram to the President of the State protesting against your sentence
on Petra's murderers?

31

JUDGE. No, no, he cannot be such a fool as to identify himself with such an outrage.

HUMMELDORF [*showing cuttings*]. You have seen these cuttings?

JUDGE. They defile us! They hang upon the edges of the city like fragments of Petra's entrails!

WIFE. What do the cuttings say?

HUMMELDORF. They say that your husband is a communist sympathiser.

WIFE [*to* JUDGE]. Monstrous! And you accept that! You don't protest. You don't sue them! You don't publicly denounce them.

JUDGE [*quietly*]. My truth will win.

HUMMELDORF. You don't realise the extent of this kind of propaganda. At the moment the life of the government is endangered. Protest meetings are being held all over the country. [*Walking across to the windows and looking out.*] I shouldn't be surprised if the Black Troops march on the Law Courts. [*Turning back.*] In your position, you are able to discriminate when you pass judgments. That is the most effective reply to the charge that you are a Red.

JUDGE. Ministers, lawyers, politicians, bishops,
All of you discriminate.
The murderer may go free, if he murders
The named enemies of your political system.
But if the passionate revolutionary
Grows violent through hunger or impatience,
The letters of the law are bars
Pulled down upon him when he slightly trips.
Listen!

32

Ten days ago, three young men were standing in the great square opposite the railway station, handing out communist leaflets, underneath the statue of a poet who stares across the square at the trains departing for the south. A police van stopped in front of them, policemen leapt out and attacked them with truncheons. You know, Mr Hummeldorf, far better than I do which side the police favour; I, as a judge, have to reach conclusions offered by the well-co-ordinated evidence of your police. Two of the Communists attempted to run away, whilst the third, covering their flight with a revolver, fired several shots. One of them wounded a policeman in the arm. Because not merely political violence but even the carrying of firearms is a crime now made punishable with death, I have condemned them all to the same death as Petra's butchers. Well, well, I am prepared to interpret the law as I have done this morning and yesterday, but there is another law which speaks to my own conscience.

HUMMELDORF. You seem to forget that the law is intended to protect the State from enemies and not to fulfil an abstract ideal of justice.

JUDGE. Do you believe that these three young men deserve the same punishment as a gang of terroristic murderers?

HUMMELDORF. [furiously]. Arguments! Arguments!
Here you sit fidgeting
At jig-saw patterns in this white, square room
When, outside, all the world in crisis
Shoots up to a prodigious firework.

33

Sir, fanciful as it seems, it is we
Who must shoulder responsibility—
Build huts against the blizzard from America,
Conduct defensive campaigns, should they prove
        necessary,
And put our shaken nation's house in order.
What are the lives of these three Communists?
Puff! Though they be innocent today, remember
Their creed draws them along a track of time
Leading to bloody murder tomorrow.
Why wait till then? Why not punish them
For your own death before they kill you?
We fought our enemies during five years,
Whole towns we bombed were innocent;
Yet now we are so scrupulous, we let
Our declared murderers grow in our midst
Lisping propaganda through revolvers.
Abstract justice is nonsense. This is war.
So kill, kill, kill.

WIFE. I agree with you absolutely, Herr Hummeldorf.
    [HUMMELDORF goes over stage and clasps her
    warmly by the hand. Still holding her hand,
    he turns to the JUDGE.]

HUMMELDORF. Sir, I have come to ask if you will retract
    the death sentence passed on Petra's murderers.

JUDGE. Then, through you, I submit to the President of
    the State that he should reprieve the three Com-
    munists whom I sentenced to death this morning.

HUMMELDORF. Even if I delivered that message, the
    President would be powerless. You don't seem to
    appreciate the situation. The Black Leader has
    thrown his whole movement into the support of

34

Petra's murderers. If the government carry out the death sentences, he will come into power on a wave of public indignation. We have only one alternative: to reprieve the Black Prisoners and, at the same time to take the Black Leader, on certain conditions, into our government.

JUDGE. Then you will give power to a man who has identified himself with a horrible murder—

HUMMELDORF. We shall have him under our control. Otherwise, we must be ruled by him. . . . The President, of course, could reprieve Petra's murderers. But we wish, as far as possible, to keep him above politics. We therefore call upon you to withdraw publicly.

WIFE. But what a wonderful man this Black Leader must be, to be able to rise above his social position —he was the son of a coal-heaver, wasn't he?—and become a member of OUR government, so filled with his superiors!

HUMMELDORF. [*elated and vulgar*]. Yes, madam,
The people united in a flooding sea
Of applauding waves waving handkerchiefs
Are behind successful Leaders who have landed
To receive power on the prosperous shore.
Any sacrifice is worth it.
Let considerations of party drop overboard
And with them all our abstract theories
And foreign logical principles.
I always say that we can waive all rules
So long as we still rule those waving waves!

JUDGE. First of all the President must reprieve the men
I sentenced to death this morning.

35

HUMMELDORF. My dear Sir! You can talk like that!
Reprieve the Communists! Let me tell you that,
within a month, to be a communist will be an of-
fence punishable with the executioner's axe. We
have to make some sacrifices of opinion for the
good of the whole country. [*Genuinely moved.*]
My dear, kind, gentle, just, old schoolfellow, do
you imagine that I would have agreed if I weren't
convinced that this arrangement is absolutely ne-
cessary?
I tell you, I have humbled myself these days.
I have been on my knees in the mud.
And, as a matter of fact, I am a proud man.
The Leader and his vulgar bodyguard
Laugh in my face and ape me behind my back.
I can see, though I am old; the old always see
That they are old, and the young, young.
They said my speeches were too long.
I was furious, and partly I could have wept
To see our world sink to its knees whilst theirs arrived
With such insolence of mockery.
I'm old, I'm old.
WIFE. Yes, we're old, we're old. Outside these windows
Life has gone past us in a tidal wave
That swept the best away, depositing
On the pavement, only conceited, bubbling dregs.
JUDGE. When I resign, I shall state my reasons for doing
so. I shall publicly demand the death penalty for
Petra's murderers and the release of the three
Communists.
HUMMELDORF. Do you approve of the three Commun-
ists carrying revolvers?

JUDGE. No.

HUMMELDORF. Then will you appeal to their support-
ers, who also carry revolvers?

JUDGE. No.

HUMMELDORF. Then to whom will you appeal?

JUDGE. To the just.

HUMMELDORF. The just! Pooh! Allow me to tell you
that the just are those who will first be shot by one
side, and then, if there are any of them left, by the
other. And no one will care.

JUDGE. How strange it seems
    That to me justice was once delineated by an inner
        eye
    As sensibly as what is solid
    In this room, tables chairs and walls,
    Is made indubitable by the sun.
    But now all crumbles away
    In coals of darkness, and the existence
    Of what was black, white, evil, right
    Becomes invisible, founders against us
    Like lumber in a lightless garret.
    I refresh myself in pleasant country
    Or I stare round faces in a room
    And although there is gold in the corn and gaiety
    In a girl's eyes or sliding along the stream,
    Everything is without a meaning.
    Voices of hatred and of power
    Call through my inner darkness
    Only that might is right.
        [HUMMELDORF *walks across to the windows
        and throws them wide open. There is a mur-
        mur of voices outside. During the rest of the*

act the audience should feel that the actors within the room have become slightly unreal; that the reality is in the street outside.]

HUMMELDORF. There is a crowd outside.
　　The breath grows from their mouths
　　Like waving flags of anger.
　　　　[*Cry from outside 'Release the Petra martyrs!'*]

JUDGE. So you have tried to force my hand?

HUMMELDORF. We have done nothing, nothing.

WIFE. For what is this the signal?

HUMMELDORF. It is the sign for a revolution
　　By those who are afraid of revolution—
　　A revolution of cowards
　　Who demand the rule of an iron hand
　　And the murder of the Reds
　　To save them from revolution.

WIFE. Do something quickly. Save us.

HUMMELDORF. All we need do is stay in power.
　　In particular, your husband can save us.

WIFE. How? How?

HUMMELDORF. By renouncing his sentence of death on Petra's murderers. By affirming that there is no question of reprieving the Communists. The rest we can do.

WIFE. Darling, save us!

HUMMELDORF. Understand that whether you go or stay, Petra's murderers will be released and the three Communists executed. If you stay, we may still save our honour.

WIFE. For the sake of matriarchy, for the sake of the barren and the unhappy who have moulded a whole strata of society into the altar of their enor-

mous grievance, for the sake of those who claim
the right to hate the sexual pleasures of young people, and for the sake of the rich and the diseased,
for the sake of funerals, marriages in Church and
the privileges of the laws of inheritance, for the
sake of the past and the dead, O hear us!

HUMMELDORF. For the sake of the authority of fathers
over their children, for the sake of the politicians of
an older generation who are elected by the people
for the purposes of concealing the real forces of
competitive power, for the sake of the respectable
and privileged survivors who adorn an age founded
on vulgarity, for the sake of our school-days, religion, the past and the dead—O hear us!

JUDGE. We are trampled beneath a brutal present
Far realer than our life-long dream
Where unrestrained new generations seemed
Always to move away as we drew near. But now
Their will grows over us making our appearances
Sham as the smiling grass on graves
Blown by the wind to belie death beneath.
Therefore, therefore my will lies
In a sleep from which the day wakes, and my voice
Which passed sentence on Petra's murderers,
Spoke in my heart locked beneath the turf
—Today denies it with a roaring gale.
I here bury my own will and cancel
My mystical hand and my unbiased sight.
I reprieve Petra's murderers and suffer those to die
Whom the time kills. Thus we who are ghosts
Survive amongst the new and potent living
To read by clearer and clearer signs

39

That day long past on which we died.

WIFE. I'm glad, I'm glad.

HUMMELDORF [*shaking hands with the* JUDGE]. Allow
me to congratulate you on your statesmanlike decision.

[*Shouts of the crowd outside 'Death! Death!'*]

WIFE [*transfigured*]. Why do they call out 'Death'?
Go out onto the balcony and let the people thank
you.

[JUDGE *goes out onto the balcony. His* WIFE
*is left alone, staring in front of her. Now, in
addition to the murmur of the crowd outside,
there is a faint drum which grows louder and
louder, nearer and nearer as she speaks.*]

The drums beat. The flags are waving.
The men march down the street.
Everything has been wrong for forty years
Because I bore no child.
But now the decorated war restores
Men to their sun and women to their night.
The young will rise from each other's sleep,
The free to be disciplined, the happy to be killed.
My huge animal body was unsatisfied
My breasts were starved because they gave no food,
My cries of hatred were as instinctive
As the babe's scream till the nurse brings its nappy.
But now I forget my self-destroying poison:
In the larger hate which destroys the world
The time is redeemed and I am content.
Let the unconsidering compact bomb cut through
Tenements and the horizontal thoughts
Of civilization. It was all false, false,

40

Only my hatred and abrupt death were real.
Let all children be killed, their little dreams
Flake like ashes under the melted girders.
I have waited for this general anger
To lance my crippled soul of poison
Till my hate explodes in war like a bomb. I am glad.
Oh, love, I'm cured, I'm cured.

> [*Three loud taps of the drum as she throws off
> her shawl and rushes out into the balcony to
> be received with an explosive burst of enthusi-
> asm from the crowd while there falls the*
>
> CURTAIN.]

Act Three

THE LARGE SCENE

[SCENE: *In front of the Palace of Justice. Railings, two trees, a street lamp, wide pavement, a raised speakers' rostrum, the shadowy building behind with faint lights in the first floor windows in front of which there is the balcony of the room in Act II.*]

[*Enter from one side* PETRA'S BROTHER, FIANCÉE *and* THIRD RED, *who is wounded: these form the* RED CHORUS. *From the other side enter the* BLACK CHORUS, *consisting of* SIXTH BLACK, SEVENTH BLACK *and a* BLACK TROOP LEADER, *dressed in officer's uniform, indistinguishable in type from the Prisoners in Act I, by whom they are joined later in this Act.*] [*The two choruses remain at their respective sides of the stage, divided by the gap containing the speakers' rostrum and the balcony above; except when one or another speaker leaps forward excitedly onto the rostrum to make a longer speech.*]

[*Although no curtain falls during this Act, the action is divided into separate scenes and these divisions should be emphasized by pauses, different lighting, etc. The scene in which* PETRA'S BROTHER *is shot recalls the atmosphere of Act I.*]

43

SIXTH BLACK. You here!
THIRD RED.   Again!
SIXTH BLACK.   I thought
    You'd been swabbed up resisting
    Our Petra blood bath.
FIANCÉE. [*mocking*]. How feed your prisoned heroes?
        Your muscular five
    Heroes, who beat to death
    One coughing invalid? How are they paid?
    How do the bankers thank
    Their hired assassins?
    What office shall be given
    That liberal judge whose conscience will fret his
        hand
    To scratch pearly as pigeon on cold pavement
    Upon their paper sentence with his pardon?
THIRD RED. Yes, yes and who repairs
    The splayed heart of your Leader
    Who sits in the South and telegraphs his nerves
    Wired across the hundred headlines
    At once with Petra's butchers?
FIANCÉE. Who thanks? And who shall pay
    Statesmen who make a literal candle
    Of blazing parliaments?
    Dons whose learning heaps
    The living leaves of art upon a bonfire
    In public squares under the eyes of statues,
    Those lenses of the snow, through death's cold
        nothing
    Staring at madness?
THIRD RED. Who pays who pays
    The doctors slick with instruments

And hiring out their minds
To castrate heritable intellect?
Whether precise with steel and frowning through
    pincenez
Or whether breeched in towering leather,
With the rhinoceros-hide whip crack
Or smiling castor oil, you are all the same.
BLACK TROOP LEADER. Take care. Take care.
    Your doom hurries. Wait here an hour
And our engine will ride the track we've laid
Under which your bodies will be sleepers.
Death answers you with your own speechlessness.
In lightless cells, in spiritless caves of hunger,
Under insult of blows, your lives will seem
Never even to have existed.
We can build history. Moles will not
Tunnel your graves; nor swallows
Fly through your trackless questions.
SEVENTH BLACK. Bullets, not speeches
    Answer such as you.
SIXTH BLACK. I unstrap my revolver
    When I hear you speak of culture.
BLACK TROOP LEADER. Or be destroyed,
    O elements of disunity, or enlist
In the army. Learn there
The inner peace of killing; touch bugle colours
Like golden ridges in the conscript's mind
Most hard and glittering at night
Under the moon and gusty flags
Which guard the deathly plain.
PETRA'S BROTHER [*leaping onto rostrum*]. Civilization
    which was sweet

With love and words, after great wars
Terrifies; architraves
Or flowering leaf of the Corinthian capitol
Momently threaten; then fall
In marble waves on life. What was
The fastened mouth of the clear past
Speaking in stone against the moving cloud, be-
    comes
Our present death. Then those
Who still will live, must tear
The spiritual will from the material
Ruling pattern of rigid memory
And the system that haunts, to hew what's real
After the living thought, not think what the dead
    have willed.
Fall marble, fall decay: but rise
Will to live, in brothers: build
Stones in the form of justice: not justice
Into the fall of funeral monuments.
BLACK CHORUS. Blasphemers against the Word!
RED CHORUS. Kneelers before dictators and the sword!
BLACK CHORUS. You, who, after this life, will suffer
    eternal death.
RED CHORUS. This life, which you would turn to death!
BLACK CHORUS. We gain life after death.
RED CHORUS. You make death in life.
BLACK CHORUS. DEATH!
RED CHORUS. DEATH! [*Leader of* BLACK CHORUS *draws his revolver.*]
        [*The* JUDGE *comes out onto the balcony.*]
JUDGE. Do not put away your revolvers.
    If you wish, shoot, I may not protest.

For I come to announce not my own resignation
But the resignation of the law.
As for me, I still wear an invisible office
And am invisible; my judgments and will
Resist you no more than the surrounding air.
When Petra's murderers heard their sentence
They heard a ghost speak and my voice which said
      death
Spoke not to theirs but from its own grave.
Petra's murderers go free. The precedent
Licenses their acts to flourish like a tree
Spreading murder which grows branches
Above that soil where the law is buried.
I scrap their death sentence.
Their release will follow immediately.
                           [*He tears a paper to pieces.*]
SIXTH BLACK, SEVENTH BLACK, and TROOP LEADER.
    This is our greatest victory!
PETRA'S BROTHER. But were our comrades also freed?
JUDGE. The same accomplished fact
    As freed Petra's murderers, sealed your friends'
      .death,
    And set a dam across my mouth
    Beyond which no Judgment may flow.
FIANCÉE. Petra's death was a crime
    Without parallel in our time.
    Yet his murderers go free, whilst for an incident
    In which our comrades slightly wounded one man
    You do not relent.
JUDGE. Not only your comrades, who will die,
    But yourselves are now a common target
    Held up by the country's laws

47

For your enemies to shoot at—
Assured of nothing but applause
When they score a bull's eye.
The most I can do for you, I now do:
I advise you to flee from here quickly.

THIRD RED. No, no your Lordship, we'll stay and shout
     our protest
Until this injustice is reversed.

JUDGE. Very well. But I must go.

PETRA'S BROTHER. No stay and join our side.
With you to lead us,
We'll form the masses in their ranks behind you
To free our comrades
And bring to justice those who murdered Petra.

JUDGE [*hesitates*]. And when the army opposes us?

PETRA'S BROTHER. We shall kill all who oppose us.

JUDGE. Then, to atone for one injustice
We create many injustices.

FIANCÉE. You have the power to choose.

JUDGE [*slowly*]. No.

FIANCÉE. You are the mask they wear
Who commit injustices and condone murder.
When their actions are most naked
And their knife flashes in an unashamed moon,
They assume your look of justice
And like a parrot you say 'regret, regret'.

JUDGE. The true face which I wear
You will see, you will see.

PETRA'S BROTHER. Now, under my eyes,
Your face changes to that face
Which is the face of Petra's murderers.
You are responsible for my brother's death.

48

JUDGE. I have done no murder, and I have saved your lives,
　　If you will accept them from me.
PETRA'S BROTHER. We refuse to fly; and what you have
　　done
PETRA'S BROTHER, FIANCÉE and THIRD RED. You will
　　see, you will see.
　　　　　　　　[*Enter* JUDGE's WIFE *onto balcony.*]
WIFE. 'Death,' 'death,' they cried.
　　The sun, which lost our Empire, now does rise,
　　And when it sets again
　　It will set in another dawn
　　Where it gilds Africa for us.
PETRA'S BROTHER. Justice and Liberty are now mortally
　　injured!
WIFE. Darling, darling, I'm cured, I'm cured.
　　It is a miracle.
　　I was so ill, bed-ridden until
　　I heard the people cry out 'Death!'
　　The dear old days are back and everything will
　　　　soon be altered
　　With soldiers marching down the street.
　　My people, you will fight again
　　Behind a disciplined nation
　　To regain
　　All that we've lost of land and ocean.
JUDGE. Dear, the night is turning cold,
　　I think we should go in.
WIFE. I won't do as I'm told!
　　These brave, brave boys are going to win.
　　I feel myself a girl again.
JUDGE. To whatever place I turn my sight,
　　I stare at my own weakness

Which brings down a Polar night
Groaning with more than winter-long distress.
These nightmare-calving fields of ice
Through black air challenge my eyes
Which can filter out no dawn
From a tired, deceiving brain.
It is time to go in.
I have worked for many hours.
Dear, come back into the house.
Lead on.

> [*Exeunt, from the balcony,* JUDGE *and* JUDGE'S
> WIFE. *The Five Prisoners of the First Act are
> released and join the* BLACK CHORUS.]
> [*The* BLACKS *approach the* REDS *threatening-
> ly, who draw involuntarily to one side of the
> stage.*]

BLACK PRISONERS. We regain our liberty!
SIXTH BLACK, SEVENTH BLACK, and BLACK TROOP
    LEADER.
    Which is the signal of victory.
The world with all its riches springs towards us!
BLACK PRISONERS. Idealistic walls fell before us!
SIXTH BLACK, SEVENTH BLACK, and BLACK TROOP
    LEADER.
    Our light floods the machinery of State power
    Now. The lever craves the hand of the Leader.
BLACK PRISONERS. Plunged, plunged in our prison
    cells of yesterday
Is the indecisive and agitating hour.
FIRST BLACK PRISONER. The time of action strikes.
    Under the windows of this judge
    Let us establish the accomplished fact

Of our right to kill Petra
And again all such as Petra.
SECOND BLACK PRISONER. We affirm our victory now
or lose!
THIRD BLACK PRISONER. Hurry, hurry, hurry,
Whispers rise from the malarial swamps.
Plotters meet in cellars. Our secret enemies
Cross frontiers and join those who ring us round.
Anger gains pressure like steam under a dome.
Sleep slides away through greasy darkness
And makes the night of all our leaders
A prison where guards beat a drum,
Commit the irrevocable outrage quickly
And found religion on it.
FIRST BLACK PRISONER. Hurry, hurry, hurry,
Kill one of these, the bitch preferably,
Just as we smashed the Polish trash Petra.
Then call down judgment
From the stuffed brain of this judge, our tame
partridge,
Who released us but holds back the Communists
For death tomorrow. His heart that broke
Once today, we'll crack under our fingers
Every morning, making it squeal
Approval to a law of murder.
Now shoot.
PETRA'S BROTHER [*jumping onto rostrum*]. Do not dare
touch any one of us. We have come here, using our
legal right of free assembly, to make our protest
against the savage death sentences passed on our
comrades. We have offered no provocation: who-
ever attacks us, will be committing a criminal as-

sault. We are protected by the laws of the democracy and by the police.

BLACK TROOP LEADER. Comrade, comrade, see how
Everything is altered.
We who did violence stand here free
And honoured, whilst your companions perish.
The example of Petra's corpse
Shot and beaten with rods, is shown
Not as an exhibition of shame
But as what the law approves. Gunmen and gangsters
Are set free, whilst bars and manacles
Exist to guard them from their critics.

PETRA'S BROTHER. Then, standing under his windows,
We appeal directly to the Judge.

THIRD RED. Yes, we appeal to the Judge. He loves true justice but his office is bound in the same chains as bind our lives. When he understands this—as he must now—he will be on our side.

[*The* JUDGE *appears in the window behind the balcony. He is not seen by the Choruses.*]

FIANCÉE. He said that he had done no murder. He offered us our lives which you would now take away.

THIRD RED. We call upon him that, later, he may call upon us to establish true justice for the people, founded on the strength of the people.

PETRA'S BROTHER. The mountain streams that have electric roots
The stones
And metals, all of them our plant;
We'll tear from where they stick in lives
Now their possessors; give them as a prize

52

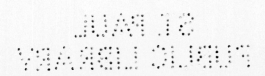

To those who've worked in fields and factories
For many centuries.

THIRD RED. We shall form a united front with the Judge
to punish the enslavers and murderers of the people and to reprieve those who are the people's true
representatives.

PETRA'S BROTHER. Into the image of a heart
That feeds separate functions with blood they need
For what they make, we'll shape the wealth
Of the dispossessed world and let those riches pour
Their fertilising river delta
Across the starved sand of the peoples.

SIXTH BLACK. Your judge has no power! His law is
founded on weakness. His rulings are not backed
by armies.

FIANCÉE. He still has the police with whom to keep
gangsters in order.

FIFTH BLACK PRISONER. Oh! Oh! The police are on our
side. Power calls to power and answers.

FOURTH BLACK PRISONER. Even the Judge secretly sup-
ports us. We can save him from your revolution!

[The JUDGE opens the French windows, but
does not go onto the balcony. The Choruses
see him.]

PETRA'S BROTHER, FIANCÉE and THIRD RED [severally].
Your Lordship! Your Lordship! Petra's murderers
threaten to assassinate us in the square. Protect our
legal right of free assembly! Unite with us to establish free speech and democratic law!
Justify your impartiality!

[The JUDGE goes back into the room and is not
seen.]

53

BLACK CHORUS [*mocking*]. SILENCE!
                              SILENCE!
                              SILENCE!
  Now we unstrap our revolvers.
RED CHORUS. Kneelers before dictators and the sword!
BLACK CHORUS. After this life, you shall suffer eternal
      death!
RED CHORUS. This life, which you now turn to death!
BLACK CHORUS. We gain life after death!
RED CHORUS. Your life is our death!
BLACK CHORUS. DEATH.
RED CHORUS. DEATH.

> [BLACK CHORUS *fire.* PETRA'S BROTHER *falls.*
> *Half-lights of illusion and uncertainty, recall-*
> *ing the First Act.*]

PETRA'S BROTHER. I am wounded.
FIANCÉE [*runs to his side*]. Where are you hurt?
PETRA'S BROTHER. Here in my chest. It seems
      That like Petra, my brother, my last thoughts rise
      From blood-corrupted lungs.
      The lungs are weeds which wrap around our hearts,
      And if our hearts have pity, today they bleed.
FIANCÉE. Stay with me and be happy.
PETRA'S BROTHER. Do not say
      I was unhappy. I built my mind
      In the foundation of that world
      Which grows against chaos and will be happiness.
      My mind's own peace and my material interest
      Centred in a philosophy of unfearing crystal
      Whose radius is the peace of cities, and brilliance
      Lack of jealousy between men.
THIRD RED. Petra, you and your brother die as heroes.

54

PETRA'S BROTHER. Is the eye heroic,
    Lying soft in the face as reed-fringed pool,
    Because for perceiving it looks to light
    And rejects shadowy obstacles
    And cuts through night like a diamond to the
        moon
    And has patience to stare a million years
    Back to the sun clocked in primitive time?
    Or is the mind heroic
    Being boxed all life in prisoning skulls,
    Lurking like a spy remote in the brain beyond dis-
        section,
    Because it has travelled further North than ex-
        plorers
    And does not freeze in interstellar space?
    Eye sees what it sees, the mind
    Knows what it must know.
    Do not say I was a hero.
    I used simply my eyes, I perceived
    With my mind, my deeds sprang
    From the sensible will.
FIANCÉE. But we snatched love—
PETRA'S BROTHER. From death—
FIANCÉE. Between death and life
    Our love shall create a link—
PETRA'S BROTHER. Yes, curled in your body, my broth-
    er's child.
FIANCÉE. We'll tear love—
PETRA'S BROTHER. From the iron assertions of the
    time—
FIANCÉE. Between the slogans of comrades—
PETRA'S BROTHER. After the ten hours' day in the fac-
    tory—

FIANCÉE. We forced love—
PETRA'S BROTHER. To grow in improbable places—
FIANCÉE. Under the street doorways—
PETRA'S BROTHER. The yawning railway arches—
FIANCÉE. One night of release in the park—
PETRA'S BROTHER. Under the trees blossoming with
      electric flowers—
FIANCÉE and PETRA'S BROTHER.
   Petra's child will be fruit of our will.
PETRA'S BROTHER. As the helmeted airman regards
   Through the glazed focus of height
   The bistre silent city abandoned like a leaf
   With veins in microscopic detail beneath him,
   So from my towered pause of death,
   O sweet carrier of life, my riveted eye looks
   Thirty years forward when our child is grown.
   Imagine if the children of this hour
   Grew free of the treelike shadows of their parents
   Falling across them with the fate of envy
   And with roots of greed that clutch their hearts.
   O leaves in sunlight, O more fortunate houses,
   O faces in the street, O lights . . . I die . . . [dies].
FIANCÉE. O, my dear love!
SIXTH BLACK [from the darkness].
   Now kill the others and say
   These were all shot when escaping from us.
FIANCÉE. [rising from PETRA'S BROTHER's side].
   Stop! Stop!

               [They stand back, silenced.]
   When Petra slept with me,
   I held the whole of life, but now that earth
   With all its trees and lakes has turned away its side

And I am left in a cold space
Which is drained entirely of the two I love.
How can I work with friends or shoot my enemies,
Since if I measure population
Against these brothers, though they're dead, they
     live for me
More than the world and all survivors?
Your clever bullets which streamed through them
Puts out the universe where it hung in their minds
And future time; for me who stay
Its comet lays waste forest tracks of meaning.
No remote caverns, untrodden spheres, delayed
Epochs, hold them where the heel may quicken
And our souls meet in music.
Throw down your revolvers. Your violence runs
Along rigid lines to destroy each other.
All we need is love. And yet we play
The meaningless game of a machine
Running in grooves laid down by death.
Go home and let me cry.

> [A low drum. Enter PETRA'S MOTHER. She
> stands above FIANCÉE who leans over the
> body of PETRA'S BROTHER. Spotlight on her
> and FIANCÉE. The rest of the stage in darkness
> through which loom the silent figures of the
> BLACK CHORUS.]

MOTHER. Beloved sons,
     You start on that difficult journey
     Away from light and towards the light
     Where the black, plumed cypress burns invisibly.
     You are forgotten and remembered
     When Spring the tiger

57

Breaks the bones with clawing roots
And the worm of oblivion your flesh eats.
But between the cypresses
The roads lead to my heart,
You are born again in the womb
Where love remembers.

    [*Enter* JUDGE's WIFE *who stands beside the*
    MOTHER, *over the* FIANCÉE.]

FIANCÉE. Terrible woman, I do not know you.
WIFE. My husband has not slept five nights.
   He sleeps now. I shall not
   Wake him for anyone. You are an inconsiderate,
   Hard, selfish generation. I am very glad
   That, when you feel at all, you are unhappy.
   The younger Petra's killed; that's good:
   Someone at last is taking measures.
   You need not think I am shocked;
   I am not afraid of corpses, having nursed
   Our brave sodliers in the War.
   They were more grateful than any of you, but they
      died.
   Get up, foolish girl. Don't ask my pity.
   You have never been through the brazier of love.
   You only miss a physical enjoyment
   Then cry like a child for a little painted doll.
   And you, old woman, why should I give you money
   Because your sons are dead? They were both scoun-
      drels.
   I do not ask for pity though I've never had
   A son; and for that I could weep.
MOTHER. Beloved sons,
   When my love too at last forgets

And the spirit attains earth's total night
Then death is complete,
The body forgiven
The soul born again;
God remembers
Those whom the world forgets,
And then the dawn of life breaks.
WIFE [to FIANCÉE]. I think I hate you more even than
        I hated
That man who, being dead, you will not marry.
At the end of his road there was a bullet!
Of yours, yourself weeping with self-pity.
I think men are fools to spare women
Who, when they hold opinions, are the worst.
If someone here should kill you, I have heard
And shall see nothing.
                        [Exit.]

MOTHER. Pity me that my second son
    Has gone to join the older one,
    I have no young strength to lean on.
    If for age you have any pity
    Of your charity throw me a little money.
        [Exit MOTHER. Enter JUDGE, from below.]
JUDGE. I have seen everything. I saw
    This Petra murdered and I looked
    Back into that brutal night now past
    Where the elder Petra lies: and then as if
    Those who were indeed poor in fact had funerals
    I saw my own weakness as a hinge
    On which the law turned to seal their deaths.
    My mind no more dwells in printed codes
    Ordered to peaceful judgments like a poem,

But in a cold dark vault, under a court
Where justice is murdered: and in cells
I see the trampled bodies of the dead
And hear the living shriek: and those
Who are the most disfigured, I yet recognize
As the most just: and from this vault
Run corridors through tall perspectives
Of future years until they break their shafts
Into a gaseous air amongst the scalding ruins
Of cities. Oh but
Everything will be changed—now I retract
The reprieve of Petra's murderers,
And I order the arrest of those who shot
Petra's brother here; and those
Three communists who were unjustly sentenced
My Court will try again.

> [HUMMELDORF *and the* JUDGE'S WIFE *appear on the balcony. The* JUDGE *standing on the raised pavement in the centre of the stage, with the balcony above him, and the* CHORUS-ES *below on either side, is, as it were, at the centre of a wheel.*]

HUMMELDORF. Sir, your resignation is accepted.
I myself, as Minister of Justice
In the National Government, have the painful
    duty
Of telling you that you are superseded
And that now you exceed your authority.
WIFE. Your wise and considered retraction of yesterday
Is the foundation stone of our coalition.
For that we are grateful and you will receive
    recognition.

HUMMELDORF. Yet we are very sorry
    To note that your unstatesmanlike liberal vice
    Of wavering at the moment of decision
    Has led to a distortion of your vision.
WIFE. There are a few of us
    Who, when the nation called, put on high office
    In the same spirit of pure self-sacrifice
    As the humblest private doffs his life for his coun-
        try in the field.
HUMMELDORF. Of course, some voices will be raised
    To claim we acted from self-interest.
    Scoffers and grumblers are ever ready to
    Attribute the base motive not the nobler.
    That is the price we have to pay.
WIFE. But you have chosen an easier and more popular
        way.
JUDGE. Oh but that when
    These griefs that bite our hearts have come, they
        come
    Lacking all dignity. I am scampered over by rats,
    I mine no genuine vein of sorrow, my heart cracks
    Alone and sterile because it is alone,
    My thought has no general meaning,
    My soul no root in this humanity;
    Nor is there God or Satan to break
    My final cry against. I envy, I envy
    Those who had faith in the past to work the good
    Or evil which they willed; who, when they died,
    Had penetrated to the core of snow
    Whose total freezing field their enemies invoked
    To annihilate them. But we
    Who are princes or ministers today, are only paint

61

On the town face of a commercial whore;
And if we are so mad as to imagine
That we control our offices, we learn
How we are nothing: our lives drop like mummies
Of the Egyptian past exposed to the real time.
FIANCÉE. Yes! Be like Christ!
Stand there, time's martyr, with your thin
Sexless body stripped, and the protruding ribs
Scarred on your side like weals of whips.
Let your self-pitying eyes sink
Deep into their bone wells and stare
At the world's tragedy played out in that one skull.
Let the iron outward spear
Knock at your heart in vain; your answer is the
     same
To those who kill you, as that you gave my lover
—Blood and water and death!
THIRD RED. For Christ also
With his great death betrayed
Humanity he might have saved.
FIANCÉE. Since when, his Church holds up a golden
     bowl
In which the innocent fingers wash away
The world's guilt from the purified soul.
JUDGE. I live and die in a vacuum
Of misery without a name.
BLACK TROOP LEADER [leaping forward with a flag].
Ring all the bells, hang out the flags,
Amaze Europe with proclamatory acts
Break through the streets like a waterfall
Armies of men, destroying all
Twigs and voices of opposition

With insuperable derision.

[BLACK CHORUS *close round the* JUDGE, *as at
the end of the First Act.*]

CHORUS OF BLACK PRISONERS.
The people hear our voice
The people approve our sentences.

SECOND BLACK PRISONER. We demand our right
That we should judge this judge
By whom we were condemned.

HUMMELDORF. The people's justice is the servant
Of the people's wishes;
Take him away: and the others too.

BLACK TROOP LEADER [*from his prominent position
now on the rostrum*]. The world we conquer must
corrupt our souls.
Its mineral veins will pour into our blood
Making the will iron. Our language
Will be the bomber's drum on the sky's skin.
The quickly conquered spaces
Will empty on our minds making them sterile
As deserts from which music is banished.
The population will be soldiers,
Innumerable, shifting and permanent in their vast-
ness,
Terrific, like sands.

CHORUS OF BLACK PRISONERS. Till now all have feared
power but we shall use it.

SIXTH BLACK, SEVENTH BLACK, and BLACK TROOP
LEADER.
With terror and violence we shall abuse it.

[*As the* JUDGE *and* REDS *are led away prisoners, there falls the*
CURTAIN.]

63

Act Four

THE TRIAL

[SCENE: *The Curtain rises on three of the* BLACK
PRISONERS, *their arms linked together. They give the
impression of being hilariously tipsy. The stage is empty
in front, with benches rising in tiers behind. In the centre (corresponding to the place of the speakers' rostrum
in Act III), there is a carved Judge's chair.*]

> [*Just as Act I is a dream in the Judge's mind,
> this act is Hummeldorf's dream.*]

THIRD BLACK PRISONER. Heads will roll. Blood must
flow.

FIRST BLACK PRISONER. Your Lordship, we find all the
prisoners guilty.

SECOND BLACK PRISONER. Discretion, my friend, discretion. You and I, who are in the confidence of the
government, we know they're guilty, but we don't
say so till we've tried them.

FIRST BLACK PRISONER. Steady, steady, steady. In my
opinion, that's a very tendentious thing to say . . .
the sort of bastard impartial thing a Jew might say.
Guilty! Of course they're guilty! Apply philosophy
to the question. Point One: *All other races are inferior, qualitatively, biologically and meta-physi-
cally to our stock.*

THIRD BLACK PRISONER. [*monotonously*]. Blood must
flow. Blood must flow.

FIRST BLACK PRISONER [*continuing, in a lecturer's*

65

voice]. Our Science, which differs from decadent,
Jewish, international science, in being biologically
scientific—Point Two—*on account of the racial
purity of the scientific workers themselves*, tells us
that we are descended directly from the Greek
Gods, whereas *they* belong to another race of *objects*—nails, chairs, stones, *things*, that is to say.

THIRD BLACK PRISONER. Heads will roll.

SECOND BLACK PRISONER. Nails, chairs, stones, bitches,
swine, objects, Jews, nothing. Blood will flow.

FIRST BLACK PRISONER. They're nothing, which is the
same as to say—Point Three—*The Jews are whatever we think they are: they are just bad dreams in
our own minds*. Without us, they don't exist: with
us thinking so, they're all shadows plotting to kill
us, whispering like birds in the branches of the
trees. [*Becoming hysterical.*] Yes, kill the Jews,
they suck our blood and defile our daughters. Kill
the liberals, who make us ridiculous in the eyes of
the world. Kill. Kill these shadows quickly, before
they overwhelm us in their universal night of chaos.
Kill them, like that [*taking a leather whip from his
belt, he lunges at a shadow*]. You see, they don't
exist, the perfidious swine. *Truth is only relative:*
That's Point . . . —where am I? What did I say?

THIRD BLACK PRISONER. Blood must flow, I say. Blood
must flow.

FIRST BLACK PRISONER. Steady, steady, steady. [*Suddenly becoming maternal, he pats* THIRD BLACK
PRISONER *on the shoulder.*] There, there, my man,
don't worry. Blood *will* flow. It's written in the
Party Programme.

66

SECOND BLACK PRISONER. Then what do we find the
    Judge guilty of?
        [*They move to the front of the stage, becom-
        ing idealized, as in Act I.*]
FIRST BLACK PRISONER. Guilty of dishonouring the
    cause of our heroic dead!
Honour War and blood of soldiers, wet-
gushing from the khaki plain, made flat
With four years of violence and of rain.
Weep for the betrayal of our blonde straight stem
Of heroic men,
By ringleted, dark, sly men,
Emigrants from the East and parasites
Who wear red, wave red flags and refuse to pour
    their veins
  Into our world-conquering sacrificial stream.
SECOND BLACK PRISONER. Stabbed in the back, our war-
    riors were betrayed
Since when, chains have bound us for many years
Of slavery worse than conquest: years of secret
    despair
Tunnelled under feather lightness of the dance
    hall and the bar.
THIRD BLACK PRISONER. Stare North, East, West, and
    remember
Shame of our countryside, shame of our corn,
Confiscated territories, self-sunk battleships,
Gangrened corpses, colonists forced to foreign
    allegiance,
Shame of vines, coal and iron exiled beyond our
    borders
By the pernicious Peace Treaty signature.

FIRST BLACK PRISONER. Prairie dogs have ravished our
    flesh and our bones
  The sword has scattered, but O they will re-assemble
  Into a brittle and pitiless army
  In death's hollow valley at the word of order.
    [*Enter* HUMMELDORF *in the robes of the*
    Judge. He goes to the Judge's chair.]
HUMMELDORF. Bring in the prisoners.
    [JUDGE, FIANCÉE *and* THIRD RED *are brought*
    in, accompanied by BLACK TROOP LEADER,
    the JUDGE *with his hands tied to a stake which*
    is planted into the front of the stage. FIANCÉE
    and THIRD RED *are put behind the Prisoners'*
    Bar, which is near the benches.]
HUMMELDORF. Regret. Let me remember. Regret.
  I do regret a change made in the law,
  Which, acting retrospectively, makes your crime
  Punishable with death.
JUDGE. I wish to make a protest.
HUMMELDORF. Silence! You will not speak until you
    are called upon to do so. . . . I declare the session
    opened.
THIRD BLACK PRISONER. Let him speak! Give him
    enough rope to hang himself with!
HUMMELDORF. Silence!
SECOND BLACK PRISONER. Who are you, to say silence
    to us?
  We are the Judges
  Who sit upon the Bench to judge this Judge.
FIRST BLACK PRISONER. You're a mascot, a stuffed bird,
    old wind-bag.
  Mind how you behave, and obey our orders.

HUMMELDORF. I have come to interpret the new law
  Which was made, I think, to press the State
  Back to the true source of its power
  Which is the strength of those who hold power,
  Expressed in the will of a Leader
  To build an army and establish order.
  My patriotism is so sincere
  That, for the land, I have come to sacrifice
  This man—my friend—whose only weakness
  Was his faith in an absolute justice
  Beyond the State and beyond the law,
  Existing in the truth of his own eyes
  Without the compulsion of the police.
  Now let the individual fail
  And the State have revenge
  And order build its army.
THIRD BLACK PRISONER. Then watch well the fate of
  that other Judge, who interpreted his conscience
  too faithfully.
FIRST BLACK PRISONER. You are brought here to see
  what happens to Judges who forget that they are
  the servants of the national will.
SECOND BLACK PRISONER. This was the old fool who
  said that our Leader would be in chains so long as
  he himself remained in power.
HUMMELDORF. Gentlemen, gentlemen,
  We are bound each to each by many chains
  Of our own interest; they bind me to you
  And bind you in the centre of your power.
FIRST BLACK PRISONER. Slave, slave, see who is in chains
  now. Observe the whip [producing whip]. Obey,
  obey. Get on with the trial.

HUMMELDORF. [*ingratiating*]. Certainly, gentlemen, I
    am the instrument of the People's Justice. [*To
    JUDGE.*] You may now make your protest.
JUDGE. I am tied to a stake
    And honoured with the superstitious awe
    They saved for witches in the Middle Ages.
    At night my hands are chained together
    My feet chained to a pillar
    In a stone cell under the ground
    Where I am brought only bread and water.
    Meanwhile, the newspapers,
    Which my ironic gaolers read me
    Outline my criminal treachery, discovering
    That my house is stuffed with bombs,
    My attics equipped, I think, with aeroplanes
    And that two battleships float like ducks
    Upon a little pond in my garden.
    It is my last luxury to laugh: and you,
    Whoever wishes, may laugh also.
    But the dumb people fed with lies
    And living in crazed darkness accept
    The least credible lie as the most true
    Which mirrors on this night of day today
    The repetition of that terror
    Which is their waking life and world.
HUMMELDORF. Release him from his chains.
        [*The* JUDGE *is released. He steps to the front
        of the stage and addresses the audience.*]
JUDGE. I speak from the centre of a stage
    Not of a tragedy but a farce
    Where I am the spiritual unsmiling clown
    Defeated by the brutal swearing giant

70

Whose law is power, his order
Nature's intolerant chaos;
Here my defeat shows bare its desert
In which emptiness wins and force levels
Wastes meaningless except to mockery.
Laugh if you will at the mind's and body's weak-
    ness
Yet if you multiply my single death
By all the deaths for which it is one precedent,
You see in my fall the fall of cities,
In this my innocent injured protest,
The massacre of children; in the triumph
Of those who hold me here
Your history clamped in iron; your word ground
Beneath the oppression of an age of ice.

HUMMELDORF. What is the charge against this man?

> [*At this question the* BLACK TROOP LEADER
> *comes forward reassuringly; as he makes his
> speech, he strolls about the stage with the re-
> assuring gestures of a middle-class holiday
> maker, occasionally practising a golfing
> stroke, or casting nautical glances from an
> imaginary sea front; that is, except when, as
> the dialogue indicates, he momentarily for-
> gets himself and becomes threatening.*]

BLACK TROOP LEADER. Before I say anything else, I
want to repudiate emphatically the suggestion that
there is anything sinister or alarming about us. It
is necessary to expose this insinuation in its vile
nakedness and state [*glaring round suspiciously*]
that we know there exist certain evil international
forces, directed mostly from abroad, which are

anxious to calumniate us, to undermine the simple faith of the man in the street who never doubts us, for the sake of whose child-like trust we are determined to root out these mockers and grumblers with the utmost severity.

SECOND BLACK PRISONER. Nails, chairs, stones, bitches, swine, objects, Jews, nothing.

BLACK TROOP LEADER. As a matter of fact, we're ordinary, decent, bourgeois people—most of us happily married and myself, I may add, the proud father of six. Most of us own a little scrap of harmless property, a small shop with a bell that tinkles happily to summon mother when you open the door, or an acre or so of land, perhaps even a vineyard with the soft tendrils of the grapes and the fine globular fruit clustering around the ripe cheeks of our laughing children and young wives. Our pleasures are in healthy exercise that breeds a fine race of manly soldiers, and in the use of our few proud possessions; in playing the piano or taking a brisk drive with all the family in the little four-seater. But we still have a pride—however little we reck of possessions—a pride in our standard of living, a pride in our little property, a pride in this nation which we dream of as our own.

THIRD BLACK PRISONER. Yes, and when our rights are challenged, we fight to kill. Heads roll, blood flows, that's it.

BLACK TROOP LEADER. We are the same stock as those who went forth to the War, many to give their life-blood for Caesar and country. Our Crusade is one with theirs. Yet this new enemy against whom we

72

bear arms is worse, far worse than those olden chivalrous enemies of rival nationhood fought in many a battle by our fathers; for we fight dragons, decadence, monsters, an evil which threatens the very foundations of our civilization. We went forth: and lo, already we return as victors. At the first assault we have slain the dragon in our land. It remains only that like a knight-errant of old guarding the honour of some distressed damsel, we go forth to save other nations—if need be against their will—for the common weal of civilization.

SECOND BLACK PRISONER. Blood must flow.

THIRD BLACK PRISONER. Now I'm telling you, if we hadn't done what we had done yesterday, you'd all of you—sitting there now so safe and sound—have been the victims of bloody revolution. Dead, the whole lot of you. They were armed to the teeth, every scrap of paper we tore off them scribbled over with sinister messages written in invisible ink. In the nick of time we saved the country from a revolution.

[The Red Prisoners begin to laugh.]

SECOND BLACK PRISONER. What are those swine laughing at? [To HUMMELDORF.] Pass the Death Sentence at once—I demand it, or you'll be shot too. No. Wait. [To RED PRISONERS.] Wait till we get you out of this Court, you scum, dead or alive, it will all be the same in twenty-four hours. Lamp posts, sewers, knives, quick-lime.

[They continue to laugh.]

THIRD BLACK PRISONER [hysterically]. They don't exist, they don't exist, the dirty swine. Kill these shadows,

73

kill these shadows quickly. [*He advances towards them with his whip raised.*]

HUMMELDORF [*as if to himself*]. To establish my world
  on stone
  I grope for the foundations
  On which the past was built
  But they slide away like waters
  Whose opened surface has uncovered
  Voices of torment, faces of chaos,
  The fall of the great house.
  I begin to lose all patience . . .
  Regret. Let me remember. Regret.

THIRD RED [*quietly to* THIRD BLACK PRISONER]. Comrade, with the night these shadows will only grow longer.

BLACK TROOP LEADER. Stick to the procedure. It's the Judge whom we must try.

THIRD BLACK PRISONER. Yes, the filthy Judge!

BLACK TROOP LEADER. A week ago this Judge, whose origins, it is scarcely necessary to add, are Jewish, had the opportunity of showing whether or no he was a patriot. He had to try five self-elected soldiers of their country who, in the interests of the glorious national resurgence, had rid their country of a rat—Petra. On the next day he tried three red internationalist scum who had shot a policeman, one of our most trusted agents. True to his Jewish origins and his international sympathies, whom did he sentence to death?

THE THREE BLACK PRISONERS. us!

BLACK TROOP LEADER. And whom did he attempt to release?

74

THE THREE BLACK PRISONERS. THEM! [*pointing to* THIRD RED *and* FIANCÉE.]

BLACK TROOP LEADER. Of what crime does every indignant and decent patriot without fail find him guilty?

> [*The Court rises, all except* HUMMELDORF, *who looks perturbed,* THIRD RED *and* FIANCÉE.]

ALL THOSE WHO ARE STANDING. TREASON!

HUMMELDORF [*rising*]. Please sit down. [*They do so.*]
What has the prisoner to say?

JUDGE. That I am guilty.
For by your law, the jungle
Is established; and the tiger's safety is guaranteed
When he hunts his innocent victim,
By all the iron of the police.
I condemned to death gunmen
And gangsters, but they are
The highest functions of this society;
Except perhaps for machine guns and those inhuman
Instruments of killing
Which are more powerful even than your fangs
Devoid of pity and the human spirit—
As indeed the time may show.
Where death is esteemed so highly,
Where death's administrators are the nation's ministers,
Here in death's court, judged by death's slaves,
I should be flattered to die: perhaps I am.
You could scarcely offer a more glittering honour.
I appeal to those

75

Who have sent the ambassadors of their powers
Into this room which well may be the tomb
Of justice for us and them
Not to conceal their horror
At the usurping of law by lawlessness
Itself made into law
To justify Petra's murder.
Let them speak as witnesses
That I am killed for nothing worse
Than my indignation against murderers,
My pity for those three who did no murder.
Let them note well my tragic error
Fatal to repeat
When I renounced my public anger
Before imagined expediency.
Then let them turn their faces to a future
Of solemn words broken by rule,
Of spiritual words burned up with libraries,
And the triumph of injustice;
Of tyrants who send their messages of terror
Against the civilized and helpless.
O let them witness
That my fate is the angel of their fate,
The angel of Europe,
And the spirit of Europe destroyed with my defeat.

THIRD BLACK PRISONER. Treason! Treason! He has appealed to foreign public opinion. Condemn the prisoners instantly.

HUMMELDORF. For God's sake, wait.[*Turning desperately to the* JUDGE, *as though for illumination.*] What have you still to say?

JUDGE. Sir, amongst the clamour and the weight

Of this event which presses on the time
Like years of roots and soil above our graves,
My guilt, yes, my guilt, only my guilt,
Remains a star and legible compass,
There to read the true responsibility.
There was a river in a sky of storm
Where had I plunged my hands and torn
The clouds apart, there now would be a joy
Of peace vast as the sky.
If when I saw that sign, if when I reached
That pole on which a generation turned and all
     that space
Of geography which is our country,
If then at least I had not betrayed myself,
These still unreal acts would be indeed a dream.
I was a traitor. That is true. Because
I might have made all of this otherwise.
BLACK TROOP LEADER. We demand not only that you
    sentence the prisoner to death but that his name
    be recorded as that of a traitor in the history books
    taught to the younger generation of this country.
HUMMELDORF. [*trembling and excited*]. No. No. This
    is monstrous. I protest.
Take his life, which he will gladly give.
And take mine too: let it lie down with his.
But when his soul has found release
From the mad torments of your living Hell
You may not smear it with your finger-prints.
No. Let it go alone to face
The terrible examining instruments
Of God, or history . . .
Oh kind, gentle, just, man,

How I remember now our youth together
And its promises, all betrayed.
Forgive me. Please forgive me.

JUDGE. Herr Hummeldorf, we each of us stand greatly
in need of forgiveness, though not from each other,
from those unborn generations.

HUMMELDORF [to JUDGE]. O Sir, I follow
Where you have gone. [To Court.] Now I retract
All that I said to condemn this man.
His example leads me into a cave,
Dripping with blood, where the two Petras lie
Dead in each others' arms; their horrible deaths
Are light and healing after this Court,
Since truth sweats through their agony, and mercy
At their tomb entrance makes a dawn
Which pleads for those three others
Who were most unjustly sentenced.

> [Walking blindly forward, HUMMELDORF,
> with the lights on him, enters a world of illu-
> sions and uncertainty, where the CHORUS
> seem shadows.]

FIRST, SECOND and THIRD BLACK PRISONERS [Surround-
> ing HUMMELDORF as they surrounded the
> JUDGE at the end of Act I.]

The people hear our voice
The people have changed this sentence and make
sentences
Other than this.

HUMMELDORF. The corpse of Petra is a witness
His wounds are mouths speaking red words.

FIRST BLACK PRISONER. The life of Petra was an ulçer
We cut out of our country's body.

78

HUMMELDORF. A word was planted in his brother's
   mouth
   A will was planted in his brother's mind.
SECOND BLACK PRISONER. We tore the word out of his
   mouth
   And cut the will out of his mind.
HUMMELDORF. A spectre rises from Petra's body
   A spectre crying that my justice
   Must die or fortify itself.
BLACK TROOP LEADER [leaping forward]. Shadows,
   shadows, surrounding us. Kill these shadows quickly.
   Trust no one. [He strikes HUMMELDORF with his
   whip.]
SECOND BLACK PRISONER. Seize Hummeldorf. [Enter
   the other two BLACK PRISONERS, who do so.] Send
   him to the cells at once. Let no one hear or speak
   of him. Dispose of the Judge and the other prison-
   ers.
THIRD BLACK PRISONER. Announce that he is mad. Un-
   fortunately the session is interrupted by his having
   a fit. Destroy all photographs taken and all reports
   of speeches in this Court. The last ten minutes are
   wiped out. They never happened.
BLACK TROOP LEADER [advancing to the front of the
   stage]. If your imaginations
   Invent and publish any picture of this scene,
   Remember that the lines cut by memory
   Into the brain may cut so deep
   They kill life altogether.
   Delete those lines. Make your brains blank. Or—
   You have seen and heard nothing

79

Except the fate of those who are traitors. [*Calling
behind the stage.*] Ring down the curtain.

CURTAIN

Act Five

THE THREE CELLS

[*The stage is separated into three cells. One, to the left, is a yard, containing a tree. The second, in the middle, is a prison cell, bare, white and simply furnished. The third, to the right, is a Guard Room.*]

> [*The* JUDGE, THIRD RED *and* FIANCÉE *are seated in the centre cell, talking quietly. They are dressed in prison uniform.*]

JUDGE. And . . . And . . . And . . .
> If from the first I had done the opposite . . .
> And released the Communistic prisoners . . . And resigned
> When the aged President demanded the retraction . . .
> And if I had published the statement of my reasons . . .
> For all Liberals of goodwill to consider . . .
> And if then . . .

THIRD RED. No, no, you are neither so wrong
> Nor so responsible as you would like to be.
> Had you obstructed those loyal colleagues
> Hummeldorf and your angry wife,
> They would have swept you aside and published
> Their explanations which, not being exactly libellous,

Would yet suggest that, except for the law of libel,
Which notoriously outlaws truth,
And except for their recognition of your former ser-
vices,
Truths might come out which are better kept
quiet—
At worst that you yourself were that still unnamed
crisis
Against which their National Government was
formed:
At best, that you are insane and need a rest.

JUDGE [*smiling*]. That I am mad is perhaps true
For the truth I see is truth, or was: and perhaps
truth
As it exists in me, is mad. For what is madness
Except one's sense of final reality
Which has become an exile from his world
And from his time?

FIANCÉE. No, no, you are not that mad and glittering
snowman
Which you imagine. Simply, you are mistaken.
It is your misfortune, for which we pity you,
That being too honest for one time, you lacked
strength
To be born into another.

THIRD RED. Your tragedy
Is not a Beethoven symphony where the hidden
silence
Of the deaf genius becomes the terrible core
Of all his sound, and symbol
Of suffering humanity.
There is no suffering humanity

82

In whom your death will be the multifoliate rose
Of a Christian sunrise
Spilled on the external martyred snows.
There are no weak and meek whom you must pity
Merging in them your own identity;
As for the oppressed, they will be the strong,
Not to weep over but make weep
Those who are now their oppressors.

FIANCÉE. Our heroes—for example, my lover and his
  brother—
Are not the seven-pointed indrawn stars
The centres of their crepe and tear-stained skies,
But those for whom a freed humanity
Was their joint aim, their lives
Spent like two bullets
To achieve that single target.

JUDGE. Dear friend, your world is the antipodes
  Of the world of those
  Who seal us in this living tomb:
  And travelling there, where all seems opposite,
  Yet all will be the same; only
  Those who are now oppressed will be the oppres-
    sors,
  The oppressors the oppressed. For your
  World and theirs exist to maintain their worlds
  And truth becomes the slave of the arrangements
  Whilst abstract reasoning is treated as a traitor
  Sniped at by necessity.

FIANCÉE. Your world, comrade, is built upon a lie
  Which is the suffering of many that the enlight-
    ened few
  May pick truths out of chaos

83

Then claim 'beauty is truth, truth beauty' to justify
The injustice of the total lie
By saying it pressed those diamonds
From years of dark and terror.
THIRD RED. But our world is built upon
The freedom of the peoples, when
Those who dig the minerals for their own fetters
And build the implacable aeroplanes
The enemy aeroplanes which terribly,
Ignominiously, clutch their children;
Those who are common as the chafing seas
Equal in having nothing throughout the world,
With no nation except their poverty
And their manifold exploited powers—
Will use the mountainous strength of their own
    arms
Which now weigh down against them, to dis-
    possess
Their destructive few oppressors.
Winning is our reality; that once gained
Then freedom will push leaves from victory
And in the borderless world of the many
States and separate power melt away.
But you in fighting these our enemies
Who kill you to delete your words,
Yet see with their hypocrite mind; you disclaim
The necessary murderous hatred,
And ignore that you or they must die.
You accept gentility, plead for their approval,
Even in death you sign the martyrs' truce
Of rebels who have let themselves be killed,
Clasping the lovely flowering crown and white

Innocence of a saint's winding sheet;
You exchange your life for your murderer's bou-
    quet
And murder your own will to earn his honour.
JUDGE. Yet I believe
    That if we reject the violence
    Which they use, we gather
    At least into ourselves, that life
    Which grows at last into a world.
    Then, from the impregnable centre
    Of what we are, we answer
    Their injustice with justice, their running
    Terroristic lie with fixed truth.
    Our single and simple being
    Will be the terrible angel
    And white witness which though they deny
    Dazzles even their convoluted darkness.
    But if we use their methods
    Of lies and hate, then we betray
    The achievement in ourselves; our truth
    Becomes the prisoner of necessity
    Equally with their untruth, ourselves
    Their stone and stupid opposite.
    And I believe
    That in our acts we are responsible
    Before a final judgment, whether indeed
    Those legends of belief which made
    The traditional sky fluid with prayer
    Freeze time suddenly into a single crystal
    Where history is transparent; or whether
    Each generation is the outpost
    Of a total spiritual territory

And defeats, even of necessity,
Are defeats indeed: for they transmit
The violence and hatred which we used
Into the veins of our children, who become
After our victory, the enemies
We spent our lives to kill.

> [*Enter, to the left, in the yard, a* JEWISH PRIS-
> ONER *followed by one of the* BLACK CHORUS
> *with a whip, who orders him by signs. Fatly
> and heavily he climbs into the tree.*]

FIANCÉE and THIRD RED. Look there!

JEWISH PRISONER [*sings grotesquely*]. In the land of
bears and Arctic breezes
Cock o' the North all the ice unfreezes,
With his wooden pole he quickly unpegs
The Esquimaux bells, Minx, Skate and Megs.

JUDGE. Who are you?

JEWISH PRISONER [*sings grotesquely*]. Though he hasn't
succeeded in thawing me
Sighed the body strung on the gallows tree.

JUDGE. Why are you sent here?

JEWISH PRISONER [*whispering*]. I am sent to make you
mad.

FIANCÉE. Who are you? . . . Who were you?

JEWISH PRISONER [*still whispering*]. I was a Jewish doctor in Breslau.
I had a clinic for women's diseases.

THIRD RED. What have those filthy scum done to you?

JEWISH PRISONER [*falling heavily from tree, shouts*].
They have robbed me of consciousness!
They have robbed me of consciousness!
[*Whimpering.*] They are coming to take me away.

86

They are coming to take me away. [*He faints.*]

      [*Enter two more of* BLACK GUARD *to take him
      away; whilst they do so, from a cell behind the
      stage is heard*]

A VOICE. . . . And ye that have sinned, ye Black Guards-
    men and ye soldiers, ye that strike the innocent
    down, remember that the Day of Judgment will
    come for ye also. . . .

      [*Interruptions of hoarse laughter.*]
    For the Lord seeth all things. . . . You must not
    arrest anyone. . . . You must be good or you will be
    punished. . . . O believe my words when I preach
    unto ye, for I am Jesus Christ the Son of God.[1]

THIRD RED. And those are the voices of the world we
      leave:
    The feathered isolation in the city
    Of the adventure to love. Voice
    Of the cheap preacher on the cheap box in the park
    Furred also with sin's luxury.

JUDGE. Yet here in peace I can at last accept
    My own unnameable shortcomings, tied
    Into a moral sack, like the dumbed clapper
    Of a cathedral bell, for thirty years.
    I was unhappy and I did not know it.
    I did not love my wife and I did not know it.
    My misery and hatred
    Was the one rich fruit of her life.

FIANCÉE. I think, I think . . .

JUDGE [*gently*]. What do you think?

FIANCÉE. I think that when my lover died, his life
    Was planted in my sleep so when I wake

[1] This incident is quoted from *I Was Hitler's Prisoner*, by Stefan Lorant

87

To the gusty day, it is as though I had returned
From the desirable earth, whose roots
Still wrap about me, to a luminous cold death.
JUDGE. Poor child, your heart is locked
    Within that cold and withering vice
    Beneath the ground, which was Petra's heart.
THIRD RED. What do you think? Waiting here
    For death, what do you think?
JUDGE. The agony breaks through my veins
    Which blaze till all my being
    Has blossomed in a single flower of fire
    Where I am at the centre of the sky.
    Everything is life and is good.
    For example, Christ the brother of Hercules, with
        childish hands
    Snaps the twin serpents, which are warring nations;
    For example, Christ is Apollo and makes men
        transparent
    Seen through by his merciless disk of light.
    And through all these days
    I think often of that powerful man
    Henry the Emperor at Canossa
    Who waited four days in the snow, until the grace
    Of the Pope melted nature's fixed whiteness
    Into such blessed forgiving as the soul drinks.
THIRD RED. You are wrong, wrong. We are nothing.
        We have fallen
    Into the dark and shall be destroyed.
    Think though, that in this darkness
    We hold the secret hub of an idea
    Whose living sunlit wheel revolves in future years
        outside.

As for our lives
When they are killed they fall like seeds
Into the ground to bear the tenfold fruit
Of our purpose; thirty spring up,
O, all the statistics show, where three comrades die.
But we ourselves are husks. Honour
Is not buried with us, nor projected
On the horizon to write our names
Through that blazing instant when the squad
        shoots.
No, honour forgets
Our minds, rejects our bodies, rises
In other bodies and wears better days.

JUDGE.
        [*During this speech a drum taps, louder and
        louder.*]
Always through my life I heard
Behind the music of the summer hills
The measuring distance of a drum.
How often all night I would lie awake
Too anxious for love, whose map
Is narrow as the bed or tomb,
My spirit's map growing to Europe, gnawed
On her spirit's face by winds of space.
Only the vibrant machine on the sky's skin
Only the emigrant distress on the frontier's rim
Only the iron anger of the Empires
Were symbols of that far reality
Which through the watching door of night
Dissolved the permanence of the city.
Now those warnings of history which the spoiled
Children of the rich exiled

From their great houses and their country lawns
To the unspoken islands of the night,
Return with every wind; and the uncivilized
Insolent message from the barbarian kraal
Across the little middle sea, upon
The yellow staring triangular continent,
Beats out its message in their lives.
I have become
The centre of that clamorous drum
To which I listened all my life
Whose letters spell the time's meaning
In this prison and my death.

THIRD RED and FIANCÉE. Look!

> [*The light in the cell goes out. Enter two of*
> BLACK CHORUS *who take* JUDGE, FIANCÉE
> *and* THIRD RED *away. Enter* BLACK TROOP
> LEADER, *who speaks to the audience from the*
> *front of the stage.*]

BLACK TROOP LEADER. Those who opposed the walls of
    our advancing sea
Are crushed to pebbles. Their minds faded and
    failed
O failed and faded like flowers before our enor-
    mous tide
Whose tall wordless movement does not resemble
    history
Taught in their libraries. For we are in no sense
    ideas:
We do not discuss and cannot be discussed.
Indivisibly we ARE, and by our greater strength of
    being
Defeat all words. Yet this Judge, in the last
    analysis believed

90

That an argument would govern the state which
    drew its form
From the same sources as the symmetry of music
Or the most sensitive arrangement of poetic words
Or the ultimate purification of a Day of Judgment.
Because our manners did not fit his mental pattern
When, for example, Petra's battered corpse seemed
    unspeakable,
Simply, he failed to perceive how far we were
    serious.
Yes, in his death, his body does not sleep
In a more rigid stupor than when he woke
To the overwhelming reality of our so-called bar-
    barousness,
Which to him seemed a nightmare where his
    time fell asleep;
For all his life he had sweetly dreamed, and our
    awakening
Is his sleeping, our victorious life is his death.
But in our strength lies our seriousness
As in his weakness lay his irresponsibility.
For, in refusing to use it, his like secretly destroyed
The sources of their own power, their over-ripeness
    held out a breast
At which the blonde monster, which would destroy
    them, fed.
Their cities began to decay; green summer flooded
The last houses and factory yards; the tall sword
    grass
Cut at the steel rails of suburban lines.
Like rusting cogs, the tanned, naked unemployed
Lay on canal banks bathed in sun's white wilder-
    ness.

In cafés, in darkness, in tenements, in slums, at
  street corners,
Voices grew sharp as knives and lives cut their
  moorings.
Violence and riot flowered. But now all that is
  ended.
The great change has come which means nothing
  will change.
Established power will have power like electricity
Wired through the street by our visible army.
The bank clerk's small house, the peasant's own
  field
Will no longer lie unguarded but be furious
  property.
Raise an army. Make munitions. Build roads
Leading outwards to our boundaries like the veins
From a heart. But the distended heart is angry
And at last it will burst over Europe as a bomb.

> [*A shooting squad fires behind the stage.*]
> [*Exit.*]

VOICES FROM CELLS BEHIND THE STAGE.
  But we shall win.
Look, look!

> [*Enter the Left and Right Hand cells,* CHO-
> RUS OF RED PRISONERS. *At first they can hard-*
> *ly be seen through the darkness which gradu-*
> *ally lightens, but the stage is never fully light.*
> *They speak very quietly at first, then their*
> *chorus rises to a crescendo with the third*
> *verse.*]

TWO RED PRISONERS. Fixed in stone darkness where we
  dwell

92

With eyes starred in surrounding night
The chainless freedom of our will
Burns towards the light.
CHORUS OF RED PRISONERS. Oh light of day
 The signal be
 Of man's release
 We shall be free
 We shall find peace.
TWO RED PRISONERS. Far from our friends, children
  and wives,
 Freedom of light that strikes on leaves,
 Our thoughts melt into those whose lives
 Suffer the ignorance of the slaves.
CHORUS OF RED PRISONERS. Worker in mine
 Our hands that join
 The signal be
 Strength to increase
 We shall be free
 We shall find peace.
TWO RED PRISONERS. Your days in dark, our dark that
  wakes,
 Across the centuries and the waves
 Will join to break our chains and break
 Into the nobler day which saves.
CHORUS OF RED PRISONERS. O break of day
 The signal be
 Of man's release
 We shall be free
 We shall find peace.
  [EIGHTH BLACK, NINTH BLACK and BLACK
  TROOP LEADER *appear at the edge of the
  stage, to the extreme right whilst the lights*

93

suddenly illuminate them, and stare in rigid
silence at the prisoners. Whilst the rest of the
stage is in semi-darkness, the walls dividing
the three cells collapse, forming a sort of gable
in the centre of the stage. During this final
stanza of the Chorus, the two sides of the
CHORUS meet and join hands across this ob-
struction.]

CHORUS OF RED PRISONERS. Quiet . . . Quiet . . .
  Quiet . . .
  Whisper of leaves . . . Far, far from laughter . . .
  We are betrayed . . . The blackness stares
  With bat eyes and furry ears . . .
  Softly . . . softly disappear . . .
  No sound of strike or riot . . .
  Softly . . . softly . . .
  Softly . . .

  [Exeunt the PRISONERS.]
  [Darkness. Then the spotlights reveal PETRA's
  MOTHER and the JUDGE's WIFE, pale and
  chalky as ghosts, lolling on the gable formed
  by the walls of the two outer cells.]

MOTHER. Paid, paid, all have paid
  To their last blood
  The price of vanity.
  My sons, victims of vanity,
  Not for themselves, but vanity
  Of the belief that man
  Can overthrow systems of injustice
  And build systems of justice.
  Till their hatred of injustice
  Justified tyranny, justified murder

94

And the cutting away of others' lives
With the will's steel
Dividing the good from the waste matter.
Vanity, vanity
Of this judge, seeking integrity
In his own suffering to pierce
The core of humanity.
All, all were vain, yet these
Loved human justice
And lost justice
When the most unjust
And the most violent, won.
Yet the unjust victory
Attains its height of gain to meet
Total defeat.
All actions and all violence fail
Which ignore that God is strong
And man is weak.
    [*She leans back—crumples up almost—in an
    attitude of complete exhaustion.*]
WIFE. Great sacrifices have been made.
    Mothers have given their sons. And
    I have given my husband.
    For in death he is with us and has become
    A hero. His mind
    Was terrible, like the soldier's
    Who, in the midst of battle, knows fear:
    The flag, the slogans, the word of command for-
        sake him
    And he turns to run, but our officer's saving bullet
    Seals his death to our glorious fate:
    Yet in that instant his severed heart

Had opened to an eternal truth of terror
Outside our time, realer than all his experience.
My husband had the courage
Of those with the true vision of cowardice
Who dwell amongst the roots of darkness
Compared with which darkness is a flower.
Through what space, amongst what spheres—
It is healthier not to look where he has looked.
[*With real sentiment.*] Therefore, my poor dear
    lamb was sacrificed.
[*Bravely.*] But I comfort myself that his dream has
    come true.
How he would love to have seen
The soldiers march towards the boundaries,
Our men's faces in uniforms all one face,
The face of those who enter a wood
Whose branches bleed and skies hail lead.
And the aeriel vultures fly
Over the deserts which were cities.
Kill! Kill! Kill! Kill!
    [*A low drum, as the lights fade. Then, from
    behind the stage, through the darkness, the
    whisper of the* CHORUS *is again heard.*]
CHORUS OF RED PRISONERS. We shall be free
    We shall find peace.
                 [*Three loud drum taps.*]

CURTAIN